A Method in My Madness

I0117760

Gemma Lees

chipmunkapublishing
the mental health publisher

Published by
Chipmunkapublishing
PO Box 6872
Brentwood
Essex CM13 1ZT
United Kingdom

http://www.chipmunkapublishing.com

Copyright © Gemma Lees 2011

Chipmunkapublishing gratefully acknowledge the support of Arts Council England.

Author Biography

Gemma Lees was born in 1983 and brought up in Bury in Lancashire. She has graduated twice from the University of Bolton with a BA in Creative Writing and Writing for Stage, Screen and Radio and a PGDE in Adult Literacy. Described as a 'street poet', she bases much of her work on the people she meets as well as her own experiences. Gemma teaches creative writing and drama in schools, libraries, theatres and community settings to a variety of ages. She also performs her poetry at a variety of venues across the North West, including; pubs, schools and colleges, libraries, theatres and festivals.

Gemma works for the spoken word organisation 'Write out Loud' and co-ordinates both their monthly Middleton night and one-off performances. A sufferer of both BPD and OCD, Gemma often struggles with her writing career but her husband and carer is a constant support, in the green room and audience at every gig.

Gemma wishes to thank all of the special people who made this book possible (you know who you are)!

Gemma Lees

She's So Sick

Have you seen
Where the stainless steel teeth bit in
To her skin?
She claims she tries her best
To suppress
To keep it all within
But white and red raised welts
Spell her weakness and her failures
And each trial and torturous test
And each endless night and darkest day
I guess some things
Can't exactly be talked or medicated away
Have you seen?
It's so childish
Like school kids with compass scratches
They unsubtly display
What should be a secret shame
She should roll down her sleeves
And keep them that way
Have you seen?
I mean, how hard can it be?
Just keep the knife in the block
She should stop
Trying to shock and elicit sympathy
From us all
We've heard it
We've seen it all before
And besides, it looks so sore
Burnt, flushed and raw
I can't help but stare
Even though I can't stand to look no more

Have you seen?
Why does she have to hurt herself?
I would, like, lash out
If I were cracked
I'd snap
I'd shout and scream
Not take it out on me
Have you seen
I mean, have you really seen?
She's just so sick if you ask me.

Location, Location, Location

Everyone knows my street
'Cause it's 'round the back of Aldi
In easy reach of the chippy
And the newsie who sells booze gone midnight
Even the cabbies who run red lights
Know they can't get away with clocking up extra
miles
'Cause everyone knows my street
And the route that saves you 20p
To put towards your fags and your leccy
Tots with exotic-sounding, fabricated names
Are dragged by wrist or reigns
Down my street
"What a shame" the old dears tut
As they fold their handbags into their bust
Then return to discussing the rain
And moaning that the bus is late again
They're waiting to be taken away
Far away from my street
Behind the shelter, lads do brazen business
Buying and selling and smoking
And stubbing their cigs out on the floor
Only stopping to scrawl on the wall
That they woz ere on my street
A pit-bull tugs his owner
Past the corner pub
"It cost five tonne you know"
That's where the money goes on my street
A middle-aged, mini-skirted lush
Staggers in to beat the breakfast rush
'Cause twenty-four hour drinking

Will never be enough on my street
You always know where you are
From abandoned sofa to jacked-up car
Walking on shit-stained slabs
Barely anchored to the ground
Seeing the sights and hearing the sounds
Of black eyes and not knowing right from wrong
And that endless drum 'n' base that reverberates
Right through the bricks and mortar
And those oblongs of dirt
The Council calls our gardens
You soon learn that's all you're worth
You soon learn that's where you belong
When you live on my street.

In Therapy

There ain't no guessing why it's in Harpurhey
Where all the Mams who drag prams are on ESA
And depression clings to all the buildings
And they're Manchester's biggest exporter
Where suicidal thoughts seep between the bricks
and mortar
And knives on skin is just one of those daily things
And they eat cold paranoia for dinner
That's where I drag myself to every Wednesday
And the school kids who won't be told
Cut across the road in front of me
'Cause they don't think I have to see 'em
One, two, three times in my rear view mirror
So I know I've not run 'em over
And in a room so uninspiring I find my eyes glued
to the clock
I sit
And I tell him all of my secrets
And I tell him shit I wouldn't tell my husband
And I'm proper fucking rude to him
'Cause he challenges everything I know about me
And he challenges the status quo within me
And I don't know why but it makes me so angry
And I cry
I cry like I can't when I'm on my own
And I cry like it hurts when I feel all alone
I cry for the scars that line my limbs
And I cry for my failures, my sickness, my sins
But it helps
I don't know why or how it does
But after I've slunk off

And touched up my fucked up eye make up
It kinda feels good
And for a moment it's OK to be me
And for a moment I see what other people see
And I've stopped counting the steps
From the door to my car
'Cause instead I kinda skip
And I guess that's why I stick
In therapy

Blackpool Rock

"Welcome to Lancashire,
Where everyone matters"
That's the sign
We weren't looking at
As we left it behind, speeding past
Both desperate to be the first
To spot the sea and the tower
Strung up with lights
Illuminating the night sky
Above Blackpool's brilliant front
But just a few streets back
Where pissed-up stags fight and
Stagger spilling their kebabs
Shouting at passing stretch limos
Stuffed with screeching hens
"Get yer tits out for the lads!"
Some girls oblige
It's not a nice show
Out the limo window
That's where the paint peels
From the façades
And the cracks grow deeper
Each season from the corners
Of once grand guest houses
No longer crammed with
Day-trippers or holiday-makers
But pasty-faced babies
Pushed up and down the streets
By Mams on the Social
They don't get to leave
After their two weeks

Of candy floss and broken rock
Nowt to do but feed the slots
From a fat pot of two p's
Quickly spent up with well-practiced,
Successive flicks of the wrist
Punctuated by the odd jackpot
They always put the lot back in
Forever chasing a bigger win
Even though everyone knows
That never happens
"Welcome to Lancashire,
Where everyone matters"
That's the sign
We weren't looking at
As we slowly drove past
Our holiday over
Bag of rock in my lap
Both desperate to be
The first to spot our flat

Happy Holidays

It's all change here
We'll watch telly in a brand new
Location, location, location
They have different news you know here
And funny foreign soaps
In between the normal English stuff
We'll drink our tins on stripy chairs
Rubbing factor 5 into hairy backs
On scrubby patches of grass
Or dog shit beaches
While the children fight
And Mum screams she's had enough
'Cause the family's condensed here
Problems are shoe-horned
Into one bed chalets
With fold out couches
For when the kids are asleep
We'll share a salt air snog here
And smell the frozen seas
On our way to the daily cabaret
The drinks are on me here
We saved up all year
A tiny little bit a week
One less scratch card
One less pack of cigs
To feed the slidey machines here
And buy suggestive rock
And Cha Cha Slide the night away
On endless Bacardi Breezers
A couple of quid less on the 'lectric
A couple of quid less on the gas

'Cause next year's Pontins
Is holding us at PayPoint

Nine To Five to Kick Out Time

That's it
It's all over
The music's stopped
The bar's run dry
Once again the crowds spill out
Squinting and shouting as they stagger by
streetlamps
To which the heaviest drinkers cling
Or push past the cloud of smokers
Crowding the doors
Puffing and stubbing and moaning
About the cold and the change in the law
It's shoved them outside to contend with flocks
That break off and scatter
In twos and threes and fours
Lads like stags shoulder charge
And invite potential fights
The lass who spent the entire night
Crying and clutching on to the ladies' sinks
Now blubbs on the curb
While her girls
Stumble in stilettos
And tell her 'He ain't worth it
And those mascara tears now smeared
On your new TopShop skirt
Will all come off
In a boil wash.'
Those at one with God
Stand on corners
Around their feet lies
A good night's out detritus

Dimps and flyers and snapped off heels
And bottles from lagers shoved up sleeves
Their plaques remind sinners that they've sinned
tonight
But they knew that
As they go home with some random bloke
Down a swift donner and puke in the street
That's it
Fun's over
Eyes run dry
Time to return
To life
To real life
To nine to five
To storing up reasons
To get pissed up and fight
To cheat down back streets
And to sleep soundly beneath a stranger's filthy
sheets

Home Is

They put me in a taxi
I wasn't sad to leave
New Hall upon hall
Of pressure etched concrete faces
Eyes open on uncomfortably sprung beds
Sleeplessness encased in dubious sheets
Each and every wall ceaselessly penetrated
By midnight cries and threats of violence
"Get to sleep or you'll get a crack 'round the head!"
I needed a rest
The driver unloaded my life
A suitcase and a couple of carriers
Dumped on the pavement
Behind chained gates
Desperate for a rubber stamping
Interviewed, approved
And shown around by an old hand
Who unashamedly relayed his past
"Me Mam were on smack
Us kids were put in care
Oh, and that's the phone over there."
He pointed to where a girl sat on the floor
Matted hair and straight back
Her place against the wall
Laid constant claim to the cold receiver
Clammy hand cradling old plastic
From which declarations of absent love poured
A tower of ten p's by her side
Each token buying a temporary
Release from loneliness
Stemming tears, saving cheeks

My new room was filthy with memory
Free to clean: I scrubbed and scrubbed
Every inch stripped of dirt and feeling
Inspected weekly, nowt ever found on me
Privacy and dignity swapped for bed and board
Those little luxuries we could scant afford
Bit of cash every Tuesday, skint by Friday
A cottage industry invented
For lads who couldn't live without cigs
Smoke screen exchanges of grief
Hardened ears listening, hearing
Whilst well-practiced fingers emptied dimps
Into rinsed-out pie tins
Abandoned baccy
Found at bus stops, surrounding bins
Newly skinned, given a second chance
They put me in a taxi
A sweaty key imprinting into my palm
Empty walls, bare floors
And the freedom to
Lock all them doors
Behind me

A&E

I kinda get it 'cause the snow ain't been that bad in thirty years
And every other bed were took up with old dears
But I just slept, I weren't shouting out like the rest
I didn't need no help with washing or getting myself dressed
I weren't pissing me bed and blaming the nurse
Who interspersed skin piercing, heart monitoring care
With telling me off and making it worse
I weren't demanding diagnoses off over-worked doctors
Or shoving my neuroses in other people's faces
Like one dear's rashes making her itch in awkward places
And give grief to each tea lady as she passed
It's not like I even wanted to be there or anywhere really
Didn't exactly go there willingly
Didn't wanna be a burden on the NHS
Taking up their much-needed bed
Swaddled in the aftermath of my own doing
I couldn't remember being dragged down that path
Had no recollection of being in the car
Can't remember standing and queuing
Or sitting on piss-proof chairs
Amidst blood and guts and doom and gloom
In yet another uninspiring waiting room
Didn't have a clue how it got this far

I'd had booklets and pamphlets and waiting lists
Promises and tablets and more tablets and yet
more tablets
I'd taken enough from them
I'd taken too much of them
But he still stuck with me all the way through
Spent his last three pounds and 50p
On a card for telly I'd never see
'Cause when you've exceeded the stated dose
You can't help but sleep but he still stayed close
Was there every time I came to
Sat there all day with nowt to do, nowt to eat
On that piss-proof chair with every old dear there
Asking him when their injections were due
Or if he knew 'when me son will get here?'
I kinda get it 'cause the snow ain't been that bad for
time
And every bed were took up like mine
But I just slept, was talked to a bit, then left

Crystal Kids

One foot flat on the floor
Hands in pockets
Other foot on the wall
Eyes like petrol puddles
Huddled hoodies, faces hidden
Skinny, skilfully rolled cig
Pinched with yellow finger tips
And perched on dry lip
Crystal kids don't care at all

Crystal kids lob bricks
Glistening shards of glass
Can't pierce bravado this thick
Can't touch the depths of disappointment
The desperation of trying to grasp
Set six maths amongst sniggering
Classmates and sarky teaching staff
The shame of signing on again
Crystal kids celebrate destruction
They thrive on it

Crystal kids flick switch blades
Out and in, out and in
With this they're the sharpest
The biggest, most brave
They can make you mind how you go
And watch what you say
They'll have your mobile and your purse
'Cause their childhood got took
One wrong look at a crystal kid
And you're smiling on the other side

Of your Chelsea grin

Crystal kids are the scum the council
Scrapes off the top
Empty flats on vacant streets
Crystal kids live in houses like these
They kick down the doors and rip into walls
What the fuck does it matter
If no one lives here at all?
Crystallise the carpets
Smash the windows for the thrill
Crystal kids live Cubic Zirconia lives
On Diamondique estates
And always will

Keep Talking

I look well
But I've lost weight
I look a bit tired
But it suits, apparently
I um and ah and nod appropriately
And my ears aren't here
And she keeps talking
I'm so lucky to get up when I like
And I'm desperately trying to work out how
To explain how it can take all day
To summon the strength to make the tea
And even then I need someone in there with me
And I'm only making fucking beans on toast
And my mind isn't here
And she keeps talking
And I'm desperately trying to work out how
To describe when you feel so low
That sobbing can no longer suffice
And I just lie on my bed
With my poor bemused pup by my side
Shaking and trying to lick my soaked cheeks dry
And my eyes aren't here
And she keeps talking
I um and ah and nod in all the right places
And she could be any one of a hundred or more
faces
And I don't want to be here
And she keeps talking

You Are Wallpaper (From Laura Ashley)

I rubber ball bounce, like you said, into rooms
Flitting between faces and filling all four corners
With whatever it is that I actually am
My loudness, my brashness
My histrionic amdramness
My superficial grin flashing whitened teeth
Saturation point reached
Me, me, me, me, me

With a grace and light touch
That trickles rather than spills
You do, like you said, wallpaper the room
Exquisite textures reflecting inwards
Tactile patterns shooting for the ceiling
They warm to your hues
They reach out for you
They want to know you
They want to know you

I just swarm you
Termiting your supports
A Marabunta raid biting away
Charming then destroying all in my path
I'm a fleeting, sweeping spectacle
Leaving nothing behind me
But an artificial aftertaste and raven black
Your colours leave a stain
Louder than you'd ever dare to speak
Bolder than you'd ever dare to be
While you paper over the breaks in me

A Hot Day In Bolton

We will fight them on the benches
In the centre
It's the spot for laughter
In the face of dwindled dreams
For happy with ya lot
For kids dragged up town
We'll be Happy Meals today
As the fella on the telly promised
It's gonna be nice and hot
Mam's got her mini skirt on
It's made to make ya mouth water
It's next to nowt
She flashes her black and blue WDK legs
Everyone's got a prop
A gammy leg crutch
Or a hand strapped up
Or a Home Bargains can
Mam pours herself all over
Whoever's fella is present
Doesn't matter today
'Cause there's summat magic in the air
I feel it like the Dib Dab foaming
On me tongue
The sun will shine on us today
And leave us wanting more
'Cause it never shines for long
And just for today

It'll make us better
We'll all be better today
Than we ever was before

Sent To

I never knew Coventry could get more grey
Than on that Monday morning
When I lay on the settee
Wrapped tightly in blanky
Watching the insomniacs' BBC
Headlines ticker-taping across the screen
Too quick for me to read
But I could see the pictures beneath
A city shrouded in a thick fog
Stopped dead
No pigeons clawing
Lady Godiva's naked body
Or the stone horse she rode on in pity
No shoppers or students
No tourists snapping Peeping Tom
Perhaps the somberness had chased them all
away
The camera panned across the Cathedral
Showing a translucent tower
Cast against an impenetrable sky
I hoped they'd stopped all the clocks today
And all the kneeling, praying and worship within
How could this city ever dare to stir again?
When I'd stayed still
I'd remain here for hours
Staring at muted bulletins
And doomed weather forecasts

Trying not to picture
The devastating news
They'd failed to broadcast
Of smoke curling from peaks of flame
Spitting, crackling, caressing skin
Coating his nostrils on that last breath in

Poor Young Thing

Poor young thing on fluoxetine
A green slip swapped for her numbness
She doesn't feel a thing anymore
Only her deafness and dumbness
That emotional drone once kept alive
By painful, longing tubes and wires
Now silenced by her next of kin
A switch was switched and it suddenly died
With her grinning doctor by its side
He holds her as if his heart and her ribs might crack
She stares straight ahead at the wallpaper
Counting the spots inside the everliving flower
heads
Tears stab the corners of his eyes and slice down
his face
She feels nothing but the wet run down her back
Not even a pin prick or razor blade can penetrate
She sees the scarlet snaking 'round her wrist and
feels no pain
I don't think I can swallow that pill down again

Gemma Lees

New Location

They regenerated my town centre
The uniform mall's going to grow
And swallow up the last remaining row
Of independent shops around
If you really want to
You can study computer-generated stills
Of the scores of copy-cat stores
About to be set in neat and tidy lines
Designed to attract new shoppers
New people, neat people
But they don't know
That 'round here they don't exist
They'll get the same old clusters
Of bunking-off kids
Young lips smeared with nicked lipsticks
Stuffed into pockets in Boots'
Running and giggling
Avoiding patrolling community coppers
Pulling chewy in long strands
From between clenched teeth
Mistaking the grotesque for sexiness
Rolled-up skirts flashing their young flesh
To gangs of bored hoodies
Whose time is all spent
Spitting on the pavement
And puffing on communal ciggies
Modelling outside the chippy
Hundreds of pounds of the latest gear
Their mams can scant afford
And bragging about the sheer amount
Of beer and birds and hits and fights

A Method in My Madness

They can manage to fit into one night out
Past them the crowds of mummies
Push babes shoved into buggies
Sucking on sausage roll dummies
Or drag disinterested toddlers
Clutching the yellow handles
Of their Happy Meal boxes
These are the little girls and boys
Who only ever play with Maccies toys
Their mums avoid the lonely old dears
Who spend all day sitting
On benches outside the church
Their tan stockings sagging into ill-fitting shoes
Wearing a heavy coat every summer
And every winter getting thinner
Clasping re-usable Mark And Sparks' bags
Full of God-knows-what and waiting
For some unsuspecting person
To sit down to their dinner
To pounce and snatch snippets
Of company and conversation from them
Before sloping off to the station
To wait for a bus to take them home
Sat alone amongst the drinkers
Chugging lurid alco-pops
Snogging, shouting, swearing
Feet rocking more buggies
Shoving bottles into skriking babies
Formula dotted on once-stitched wrists
'Round here it's not bricks and mortar
That drags us all down
New shops, clean lines
Won't make new people, clean people
Won't change people

They can't change people
By regenerating buildings
By only changing the scenery
By adding more reasons to waste
Our money and time and lives away
It'll stay exactly the same
In the centre of our town

Wreckuiem

A hole in your stomach
Drip, drip, dripped black goo
I looked at you
Elevated and essentially gone
I was too scared to say goodbye
I was too ashamed to cry
I wondered what went wrong
What had I done?
I thought I took such good care
You were clean and full and loved
I missed you when you weren't there
We shared my escapes and escapades
You taught me to love the night
We spent evenings just chasing lights
Driving around with you
Just felt right
Going nowhere in particular
And I felt safe alone
You held me tight and protected me
All the way home
Everybody told me how lucky I was
To have found you
We neither were new
But we felt new together
It was just a normal day
When you started to cough
Your splutters worsened

On the way home from the supermarket
Once operated on
They wouldn't let you leave
Too far gone to fix
Too dangerous
Belongings shoved into a plastic bag
For a moment I looked back at your shell stood
there
They stripped you bare for scrap
That last drive was just a trip too far
For my 106
My first car

Cashy Gs

When you ain't got the readies
For the stuff what you need
Come young, come old
Down to Cashy Gs
Outside the mams smoke
And share stories
Of her down the road
And how they've had enough
While Daddy goes in Coral
For a sure thing
What he were told
By a bloke down the pub
Daz has his trackie leg rolled up
So you can all see his tag
So you know that he went on the rob
For all the shit he never had
He trades in his X Box
For a night on the lash
'Cause cash is king
When you're out with the lads
They photocopy your Giro
And make you shakily sign
With leaky, smudgy Biro
Then they take your picture
The one thing you can't fake
That's to check
That you ain't on the make

That it's your kid's PS3
Your own weight in gold
Your very own treasures
That have gotta be sold
And cash is hard
And cash is cold
And cash ain't got no story to be told

A Little Bit More

Mam's sunk another quid on it
She saw her reflection in the plastic dispenser
A pick 'n' mix of promises
Laid out before her
This time she'd have to win, 'right kids'?
She's got this lucky 2p
She uses ever so carefully
It takes off the silver foil
Tiny curls that fall to the floor
The corners and the edges first
Then just a little bit more at a time
She is fastidious about it
Every last inch has got to be scratched
Anxious anticipation niggles at her
She lets her imagination conjure up
The second look, the gasp, the celebration
The breathless 'at last kids!'
The first two lines are gone
'It's looking good, kids
I've got two hundred grands on
That'd sort us out
A mansion and an acre of land
Come to think of it
I'm not exactly sure what an acre is
But it sounds like what posh people get
Nice and big and, and, and…..
…..nevermind kids
There's always next time around'
Mam's always got that one last pound

Constructive Criticism

I've been criticised since I were a child
To help me out, I understand
Like when my teacher made it clear
That me chubby Crayola was in the wrong hand
As left, it just ain't right, my dear
And all the metal rulers slapped on desks
Making tiny slumped shoulders snap to attention
Couldn't make me understand Roger Red Hat or
Billy Blue
My phonics certainly weren't jolly
And my misspelt scrawl wouldn't do
I'd never come to owt and it were about time I knew
Standing outside the head teacher's room
Chastised again for my crocodile tears
To help me out, I understand
Like when, ten years later, I stopped trying
To please teachers who just shook their heads
And slammed exercise books down on desks
Best efforts ringed in angry red
Blazer pockets stuffed with nowt but letdown and
DTs
To help me out, I understand
Like when, at sixteen, pristine NI card in hand
I got my first proper job at a bakery
Seventy quid for six day's slog a week
In ample smock scrubbing floors on me knees
Scraping fat out of tins with me bare hands
Grating fingers along with breezeblocks of cheese
Making up muffins for people with delusions of
grandeur
Talking down to me to feel like butty kings

A Method in My Madness

Constantly followed, scolded, told what to do
By a boss who beat bakehouse mice with her shoe
To help me out, I understand
To keep me stupid dreams in hand
To keep me head in check and down to size
Since I were a child I've been criticised

Education, Education, Education

Is there no shame
In going along with crowds of kids
Kicking backpacks down halls
Pulling welcome displays off walls
They say "send your kids here, Mrs"
To wear our badge on their chest
To take beatings for our Latin motto
Not one of us can read
No one understands each other 'round here
'Cause there's a new modern language
To be learned every year

Is there no shame
In slouching down socks
Wearing several pairs at once
To disguise non-regulation shoes
Shirt untucked, skirt rolled up
Revealing goose pimple legs
Strewn with beginner shaving nicks
Hair stiff with spray
False nails stuck on with gobs of glue
Used for picking through food
Believing girls only eat by the pinch
Avoiding tears in a locked cubicle
Over another teenage inch
Pockets stuffed with shadow and blush
And sticky lippies screwed up in fat tubes
To put on an take off in the ladies' loos
Cheeks, lips and lids smeared on in breaks
But sat in each lesson with
A paper-towelled clean face

A Method in My Madness

Foundation plastered over acne
An orange tidemark against a white neck

Is there no shame
In that first crush on a fifth year lad
Pillow-kissing some mag pin-up
Or the youngest Sir on the teaching staff
Embarrassingly emulating the stances
And saying of pop and screen stars
Pouting and fluttering false eyelashes
Notching up another absent mark
For your first song on the park benches
Surrounded by a crowd
Of cheering, jeering girls and boys
"Go on, use your tongues!"
That first clumsy fumble
On your boyfriend's Mam's sofa
Plasters concealing a fresh hickey
Proudly flashed to your mates in the yard

Is there no shame
In acting out to not be the outcast kid
Banished to the front of the school bus
Not cool enough for the back seat clique
Reluctant sparring partners
Forced together in the centre
Of a circle of kids screeching for more
"Fight! Fight! Fight!"
Punching, kicking, clawing, sly digs
Busting noses, splitting lips
Rolling on the floor
Shit nicked in the confusion
Bruised fighters limping away
Pretending they're not hurt

Blood spatters on crisp, white shirts

Is there no shame
In taking that drag on your first cig
Appointing some wimp who won't join in
As look-out 'round the corner
Of the gym building
A smile forced through splutters
Coating the ground in spit
Protesting your enjoyment of your new habit
Buying and selling singles for 50ps
Making a packet
From the playground racket
Begging passers-by
"Will you go shop for us, please?"
Taking that first clandestine swig of cider
Under a humming streetlight
Sat giggling on the swings by day
Or hid under the slide by night
Mixing you drinks with anything
You've managed to pinch
From Mam and Dad's stash under the sink
Trying owt that's pushed your way
With a "Go on!"
Swallowing, smoking or sniffing to belong

Is there no shame
In the game of growing up
The pointless stuff we did at the time
To bridge that gap between adult and child
Indulging in the best days of our lives
Surely we were all the same
Surely there's no shame in that?

My First Funeral

There were no sing-along hits
Painstakingly picked for mix CDs
At the start of this sombre road trip
Just jabbering local DJs
Changing accents, same old chatter
As we crackled over each county's boundary
From North West to South East
He driving and me counting junctions
Passing him pop
And squeezing his hand
As he rested it on his knee
At each red light
Travelling three hundred miles
To say goodbye
To a shut up box
With our friend inside

The cool countryside church was packed
With Punks, Goths, Emos and Freaks
Drawn to this village from countrywide
Disturbing the peace and quiet
Just how he would have liked
I managed not to cry
Until they brought him inside
Everyone was wearing his footie team's sky blue
And once outside it was as if the sky knew
As even it obliged
And sky blue was all I could see for miles
Around the secluded field
Full of grey and white stones
And his box lowered into his hole

Surrounded by mounds of Earth
We stood in line
Under that blue sky
To say goodbye
To that shut up box
With our friend inside

After sing-alongs
And dancing down the motorway
We sat in his local
Toasting his memory
And reminiscing the rest of the day away
Drink blurred those unreliable memories we shared
Showing each other slightly more reliable
Memories snapped up
In still-framed longevity
And we said goodbye
To an unlocked box
We could look inside
At any time

Learning To Read

Words abandoned me
When I were at Primary
Didn't make sense no more
Like when me Dad and me
Made up stories
And created crazy characters
Like Fezzypeg
Who me Dad said were a cat
That owned a record shop
And talked and walked on his hind legs
And though I couldn't always keep in mind
Everything I was told at other times
And I fell over
And I couldn't catch a ball
Or decipher those clock hands
Or handstand or cartwheel
Or skip or do claps
Or cat's cradle at all
And I got lost
Walking down a straight hall
I always understood
All the colours and the waves
And every word's shape
They stretched towards me
Surrounded me and I heard
And from the stories I spoke
My all over the place head held tight to
Every syllable
Every sound
Illustrations never sketched
Sentences never written down

But with pencil pressed into tiny hand
Or open page etched
With uncrackable code
I couldn't do it
And they said I were thick
It didn't make any sense
Those hieroglyphs and squiggles
That tiny typed scrawl
Arranged in tidy lines
They wouldn't turn into words
And colours and sounds
No matter how hard I tried
And I tried
I really tried
I watched me feet when I were running
Practiced claps and cat's cradle
And kept me eyes on the ball
Until I realised
That maybe I were thick after all
Now time has passed
And people pay me
For my words
For my colours and my shapes
For my sounds and my waves
For my poems and stories and songs
So maybe
Just maybe
Them teachers was wrong

The Marital Bed

For three and a half years
It was all mine
Selected for being the cheapest
In the Argos book
Picture clipped and glued
To my care grant application
I was the hypotenuse
Arms and legs and fingers spread
Out in my first own bed
No strangers had sunk into my mattress
Before me
It arrived wrapped in plastic
Flat packed poles and bags
Of nuts and bolts
Clean and pristine and all mine
I filled all four corners up
Stretched out
In a sleeping starfish
Contentedly enveloped in sheets
That could never be taken
Away from me

Then I had to learn to love
Lying parallel
Fighting for covers
Keeping my feet and fingers to myself
When after initial cuddles
We retreated to our individual
Comfortable sleeping positions
Both facing outwards
Towards our own walls

Waking up freezing cold
Snatching back stolen covers
Bunched up on top
Of a hot, pink body sleeping soundly

When he was too drunk to drive
Home and kipped on a mate's sofa
I slipped into my old starfish position
Filling all four corners
With splayed fingers and legs outstretched
And woke up freezing cold
Missing the nightly fight
That means our bed may not be
But he
Is all mine

The Preacher of the Old Blue Bell

The preacher of the Old Blue Bell
Speaks in tongues
And we listen
Occasionally
He can't get falling over drunk no more
Just scraped through his twenties
Being prised off pub floors
Tried a life in his thirties but it didn't stick
Now gets dicky ticker Social
Forty six on paper
He sits
Straight backed
Usual stool
End of the usual row of
Other blokes bent over the bar
"Pint of usual and scratchings?"
The barmaid asks knowing the answer
Shaking hands push a pile of tarnished pennies
Towards her
Clasping then raising the cool glass
He squints as it catches the light
Fresh from outside
Transfixed as if it's an object of great beauty
Before swiftly downing
He's drowning and drinking to us
Sharing his slurred words of wisdom
His unlived life
And undecided opinion
He's supping till he's never wrong
The preacher of the Old Blue Bell
Speaks in tongues

And we listen
Occasionally

Rocking Glockenspiel

I wanted to rock on my glockenspiel
But Miss had only left two bars on
Not content with a droning dum, dum, dum, dum
With my baton I bashed irrhythmically
Possessed with a dyspraxic urgency
To make music with the others
But I were playing a different song to them
Lost in a perfect pitch posse
All chords played out precisely
On posh violins and flutes
And other clever things
I just wanted to rock on
But the glock was snatched from me
And I was forced to play
Triangle
With wand to cast a tune from three gleaming sides
I carried on
Even when Miss tried to hide
Me right at the back
Behind the chubby cymbals lad
And the trio of rotund cheek recorder blowers
I ting, ting, tinged my way
To the top of the tune
And before I knew it
My status was lowered again
And I was demoted to split peas
Inside a taped-up Vitalite tub
I shook and shook and shook and shook
'Til the tape came undone
And the smarmy, private music lessons after school
pack

Were pelted
Tiny split peas in eyes and hair and pockets and
trombones
Which were fun for a minute but there's nowhere to
go
There's nowhere lower than a split pea shaker
Except standing up front and holding Miss' papers
And that's how I became a sheet music stand
From standing with shiny triangle in hand
To showering assembled musicians with split peas
Not to mention the music room floor
The fourteen-year-old me
Wannabe glock rocker
Burned out too soon
And was
No more

On The 471

The 471 takes you direct from
Rochdale to Bolton
And as you sit relatively comfortably
You get to people watch the people
That you'd never wanna be
You see him who unashamedly
Sings on his own
To the top 40
On illegal download
Crackling out of his phone
And he don't know the words
And he don't know the tune
And he's wailing every word
Too late or too soon
He pulls his trackie top up
Over his chin and his cheeks
And tugs up the zip
'Cause the muck spreading outside
Is making him sick
But he smells like he ain't bathed in a week
Some burly bloke from Bury's doing business
Barking obscene orders down his mobile
He's buying and selling his gear
He don't sit quite right in his seat
Parted legs stretched down the aisle
He's the kind of fella you fear
Meeting down an alley on a dark night
A leering chav licks his lass' lobe
Swollen tongue stuck down her ear hole
He rasps not-so-sweet somethings
Tugging on her gold hoop earrings

Eyes on tits and brain in kecks
Sticks his hand up her skirt
And thinks what the heck
But he's in for a shock
'Cause she ain't like that
"I don't do it on buses,
Only back at your flat!"
Some mam's already on her last nerve
And her hand's stuck in the buggy
Kids won't sit in one place
Going flying as the bus driver swerves
Several people tut
But mam ain't fussed
She finds it kind of funny
She's neither willing nor able
To make them behave
And anyway she's busy texting her mate
Lol, rofl, smiley face
Now you've reached your destination
You've gone from A to B
Witnessed a good cross-section of society
Now alighted they scatter 'round the station
Still humming, trading, snogging
Ignoring mam's protestations
Half-hearted "nos" to no avail
If you get back on
If you really want
You can go all the way back to Rochdale

The First Cut

The first cut was not the deepest
It was nothing
The blade barely bit
Playing at slicing skin
Sobbing at that first glimpse of crimson
Creeping around my arm as I twisted it
And watched
And waited
To feel better
And I did

The first cut was not the deepest
But it dared me to go deeper
To go further
To press on harder
To grip the handle tighter
No light touch
No satisfaction at scratching
Skimming, skirting around these issues
Watching slightly sickened
Soaking scrunched up tissues

The first cut was not the deepest
But now only it will do
It's become a bloody routine
From assembling the instruments
To keeping it clean
Completing each step precisely
Stemming, stanching, covering until it can clot
Plastering it up nicely
Now I know the meaning of deepest
I know that first cut was not

She Says

She says it in a voice that isn't quite caring
Isn't quite sympathetic
Isn't quite anything whatsoever
She says, "but you are very clever"
What am I supposed to say?
Take the compliment
And walk away?
But I'm here for help
I made that huge leap
I'm ready to vent
I'm ready to dig deep
I'm ready to reveal bits
Of the real me
But she's making a meal
Out of my made-up face
'Cause she don't get I wouldn't
Go out any other way
When I don't look right
I just stay inside
'Cause I feel so ugly most of the time
And she cocks her head
And starts to frown
As she's writing all of this shit down
And I wanna look
But she says "no"
And I wanna just get up and go
But I'm here for help
And I'm ready to spill
I'm ready to let go
I'm ready to squeal
All she wants to know

But she says "but"
And she's stuck on my degree
But it ain't in being normal
And it ain't in getting me
She says "what do you want?"
And I don't know what I need
She sighs and shrugs
And says she's sorry
But until I know that
We can't proceed

Sixteen Bars of Soap

There's sixteen bars of soap
Secreted beneath my bed
Last night fifteen senseless chants
Rolled over and over inside my head
Fourteen times I waggled and shook
And kicked the locked up door
Washed my hands thirteen times today
And they're gonna get washed tonnes more
Twelve times now I checked the fridge
That the light comes on and it's cold
Eleven times I asked myself
Why my life's so fixed and controlled
Made sure ten times the gas hob was off
To keep my husband safe from harm
When I've questioned him nine times on it
I might get a few moments of calm
Counted to eight whilst tapping the drawer
So I knew the washer would work
Seven times I lied to myself
I'm alright, I've just got a few quirks
Six times I checked and rechecked texts
To ensure I'd caused no offence
I chastised myself five times for rehearsing
Repetitious rituals that make no sense
Four times I went through the drawers
To make sure no clothes were creased
Only three times I managed to cope
Until my anxieties decreased
I Googled my condition twice already
And felt like a complete freak
Just once, when swayed, I'll take my meds
And slip into a synthetic sleep

Start Something

Prescribe me not anti-psychotics
Antidepressants don't touch this ache
Instead give me paper and pens
And pastels and pencil crayons
Hours of calm in cool, lofty rooms
To sketch and paint
And make beautiful mistakes
I'll retain each failed experiment
There's no shame in here
Nowt's screwed up and chucked away
Even dried up old acrylic tubes
Are kept for their distinctive aesthetics
We draw them
And record each dent and ding
'Cause maybe there's a tiny bit of
Beauty in everything
And if you're ever gonna find it
You'll probably find it here
Between creating and crafting
Feel free to catch conversation
With anyone
There ain't no cliques
No art critics
Just tea and empathy
Toast and unspoken understanding
No pressure to discuss diagnoses
No pressure to disguise them
No pressure to produce perfection
No pressure
Prescribe me not anti-psychotics
Antidepressants don't make me feel this way

Just give me a full day
Of not just something to do
But the drive to do it too
And the freedom to Start something new

www.ingramcontent.com/pod-product-compliance
Lightning Source LLC
Chambersburg PA
CBHW031141270326
41931CB00007B/641